Paying Your Bills

The Basics

Gwen and Dennis Keegan

Images by Gwen and Dennis Keegan.

This booklet is available from Amazon.com and other online stores.

Copyright © 2018 Gwen and Dennis Keegan

All rights reserved.

ISBN: 1984926357
ISBN-13: 978-1984926357

CONTENTS

Introduction   iv

1. Getting started   Pg # 1
2. Bill paying area   Pg # 4
3. Pay bills   Pg # 6
4. Planning your budget   Pg # 9
5. Credit rating   Pg # 15
6. Some Dos and Don'ts   Pg # 17
7. Summary   Pg # 21

INTRODUCTION

To anyone who has ever struggled with finances, you are not alone. As a retired Real Estate Broker (Dennis), a retired Registered Nurse (Gwen), and small business owners (both), we have been asked on many occasions by our younger clients and friends how to manage daily finances and achieve financial stability. Buying a home of their own or enjoying financial independence are frequent goals that we hear mentioned. We decided to write down our hints and tips instead of starting from scratch each time this subject arises. This simple booklet is the sum of our trial and error in setting up our own process. It is what works for us. Modify it to work for you.

Think of your money as a pot of soup. It is not bottomless and is not refillable. Say the soup must last for a week (as does your weekly income). That is all you have, and you will go hungry if you run out early. First, you would parcel out how much soup you could allow yourself for breakfast, lunch and dinner, each day for seven days. You would need to stick very closely to the schedule or risk running out of soup before the week is over. Talk about motivation! The same principle applies to your money. Running out of money is not fun!

We hope you can benefit from our experiences. Here are some of the simple steps we have developed.

1. GETTING STARTED

Paying your bills sounds so simple. And to some people, it is. But for those who struggle with it – here are some hints that we have developed over the years.

First of all, you will need to know how much money you have coming in each month. Then set a budget for how much you will be able to spend on those things that you require and those things that you desire. It important to realize that there *is* a difference between 'require' and 'desire'. Also, budget to <u>save</u> some money each month.

It helps to make a list of the requirements for your basic needs. Such as rent or mortgage, food, utilities, gasoline, car payment and each unavoidable expense that you have. Beside each item, list the amount of money you are currently paying each month. You can go back through your checking account, look up your checks for groceries, for example, and add up what you have spent in the past 12 months, then divide by 12 to get an average (if you don't already have a good idea of what you spend for food per month). Or look at your credit card statements if you buy your food with a credit card.

Now add up the basic need expenses and compare your total monthly income (take-home pay) to your total monthly expenses. If you are bringing in more than your unavoidable expenses, that's great. If not, you will need to do some prioritizing to see what expenses you can cut back on. Or find a way to increase your income, such as working more hours, obtaining a temporary second job if that becomes necessary, or splitting chores and having all adult members of the family work at least part-time. You may need to be creative to find ways to increase your income but beware of offers that sound too good to be true, such as "Work from home, make $1000.00 an hour!" If it sounds too good to be true, it is probably not true. If you have to pay them $2000.00 for materials before you earn money, they are likely the only ones making any money. (More on jobs in Chapter 6.)

Here is a sample income and expense sheet. You can make one for yourself either with old-fashioned paper and pencil or make a spreadsheet if you are computer savvy. This sample is just to show you how to begin and does not have realistic numbers plugged in.

Over-simplified sample

Income	Monthly	Expense	Monthly
My paycheck	$1,000.	Rent	$750.
Spouse paycheck	$1,000.	Food	$300.
		Utilities	$200.
		Car payment	$100.
		Gasoline	$150.
Total income:	$2,000.	Total expenses:	$1,500.

Now subtract the total expenses from the total income:
    $2000.00
    $1500.00

    $ 500.00

As we see, this over-simplified sample left this couple with $500.00 extra per month. However, we have left out some obvious expenses that many people have. It will be important to list all of your recurring expenses in order to fully explore where your money is being spent. As mentioned earlier, it will also be important to differentiate between expense items that are *required* and expense items that are *desired*.

Later we will review a more detailed budget. First, we will discuss the actual process of bill-paying.

2. BILL PAYING AREA

First, decide on a bill-paying area to keep your supplies and bills in order. You will ideally have a desk or a surface area and a drawer or two for supplies. This area can be as simple as a corner of a kitchen counter, or as elaborate as an office desk, whatever your style and circumstances allow. You will need office supplies such as pens, pencils, paper clips, envelopes, stamps and room to keep your due bills plus paid bill receipts. Ideally you will have a file folder to keep the paid bill receipts in order.

When your bills arrive in the mail, open the envelope and note the due date. Write the 'pay by date' and 'due date' on the outside of the envelope and place the bill in date order in a stack in your bill-paying area.

```
From:
ABC Utility
Newtown, USA
                                     $34.25 Pay by 2/5/18
          To: John Dough            Due by 2/18/18
              123 4th Street
              Maintown, USA
```

We use a small upright file holder to keep the bills on our desk prior to paying them. This keeps them in sight and decreases chances of forgetting them.

Notice the due dates of all your bills and figure out how frequently you will need to pay bills in order to keep current with all due dates. Set a time that is reasonable for you to maintain. Possibly once a week will suffice.

You may be able to sit down and pay bills once a week, or you may have some that need to be paid as soon as they arrive. Whatever the case, be sure to pay each bill well before the due date so that you do not pay any late charges. Allow time for the mail to deliver the bill in time to avoid late charges, as well as enough time for the company to process and post the payment. Late charges just add unnecessary expense and <u>are avoidable</u> with some planning on your part.

This bears repeating – <u>never incur late charges!</u>
<u>Plan ahead!</u>

3. PAY BILLS

Say it is Saturday morning and this is your routine time to sit down and pay bills. Go through your stack of bills that have accumulated in the mail and sort out which ones need to be paid this week. Add up the total expenses and confirm that your checking account balance is going to cover the total amount.

Due:	Gas	$150.95
	Phone	$240.45

		$391.40 total

Current checking account balance =	$624.30
Minus bills due:	391.40

Amount left after paying bills:	$232.90

If your checking account balance is not sufficient to cover the due bills, you will need to do some prioritizing to decide what must be paid and what could wait.

If possible, always pay more than the minimum amount due on any credit card debt. This will minimize your finance charges (which are considerably large on most credit card debt) and help pay off these debts as soon as possible. Pay off the highest interest cards first to minimize the amount you are paying in interest/finance charges.

Paying Your Bills

A goal should be to pay off credit card debt completely each month to avoid those hefty finance charges. This may seem impossible at first, but when you take a good look at how much the finance charges cost you each year, you will want to be able to keep that money in your own pocket.

Now you will write out all the checks for the bills that you are paying today. On the portion of the bill that is for you to keep for your own records (your receipt), write the date, your check number, and the amount of money that you are paying. If more than one bank account is used to pay bills, write which account the check is from beside the check number. This will make it easier to tell where to look if you need to go back and look at the payment. We just put our initials beside the check number to indicate which checking account it is from, as in the mock example below.

```
              ABC Phone Company
                   INVOICE
   Date: 1/10/18              Due by: 1/31/18

   Equipment:       $7.51
   Monthly charge:  $89.00
   Taxes:           $6.24
                    _____
                    $102.75

                    Paid $102.75 on 1/18/18
                    Check # 1234 DK
```

File this portion/receipt in some orderly manner. We use an accordion file with pockets labeled for each monthly bill. You might want to use file folders, or some other method.

Just make sure the method of filing is orderly and makes sense to you. If you need to retrieve a bill receipt, you will be able to go directly to the right place. Also, come tax time you have all your receipts at your fingertips and not stuffed haphazardly into a shoebox.

As you write out your checks, be sure to keep your checkbook register up to date by deducting the recent check from your running bank balance in the checkbook register. This will keep you aware of your current bank balance. Be sure to reconcile your monthly bank statement with your checkbook register, each month, too. This way you will not incur bank charges from overdrafts or allow any mistakes to affect your totals.

Of course, you may also pay some bills online or through automatic deductions. You will want to set those things up individually according to each company's instructions. Take care to understand their instructions and be sure you aren't paying extra for this service. Also, make sure you will have the funds available for any automatic payments, whether it be by credit card or by checking account deductions.

Always go over your credit card monthly statement to be sure the charges are correct and were made by you, to detect credit card fraud right away.

You will want to make a file folder for receipts of items that you need to include on your tax return. This may be a separate receipt, a tax information report (1099) that you received in the mail, or a line item on your credit card statement, for instance. Include anything that you will need to itemize on your tax return, if you do indeed itemize (not everyone does).

4. PLANNING YOUR BUDGET

Now to discuss the issue of budgeting your income. This is a crucial step and is what trips up many people. You cannot spend more money than you make! Take some time to write down all the expenses that you have during any given month (such as rent or mortgage) and add any other expenses that will occur during the year (such as your renter's insurance or homeowner's insurance). If you are new to this process, don't expect to remember all of them in one try. Start your income and expense list and add to it each time you receive a bill or pay money for anything. Any cost that recurs should be added to the budget to account for the expense.

On the next page is a sample chart that contains some typical monthly and yearly expenses. (Divide the yearly expenses by 12 to arrive at the monthly outlay).

Income	Monthly	Expense	Monthly
(list all income)		Rent	
My paycheck		Food-groceries	
Spouse paycheck		Utilities (gas, electric, etc.)	
Alimony		Water	
Child support		Car payment 1	
		Car payment 2	
		Insurance	
		Gasoline	
		Child care	
		Credit card 1	
		Credit card 2	
		Internet/cable	
		Phones	
		Food-eat out	
		Pocket $ me	
		Pocket $ spouse	
		Savings	
Total income:		Total expenses:	
Income minus expenses =			

Add any other expenses or income that you have, to personalize this example to your own circumstances. Use a separate line for each utility bill so that you can track each one. Add any newspaper or magazine subscriptions, membership dues, church offerings, child's allowance or any other known monthly expenses. Consider things such as pet expenses, doctor visits, medical insurance, clothing expenses, gardener, house cleaner, dry cleaners, your daily take-out coffee – anything that you predictably will spend money on during a typical month. The more detailed your budget items, the closer you will be to managing your money.

Note that on this example 'Alimony' and 'child support' are listed on the income side. Both of those categories could be income to some households but will be expenses to others. Individualize the sample budget to your own situation.

For your income amount, use your take-home pay (not your gross pay), as that is what is used to cover all your expenses. Hopefully, you will also add a line for 'savings' to your monthly obligations. There will always be unexpected expenses that crop up and your savings could actually save the day! Do not include any 'expected' income, such as bonuses if the amounts are variable. You will need to budget on your basic income if the bonus amounts fluctuate. Then when your bonus does come through, you can use that money to pay down debts and to put some in savings. Do not count on money that may or may not arrive until you actually receive it. Similarly, do not write checks before the money is in the bank, thinking that you will 'cover' it before the check gets cashed. If you don't make it to the bank in time, or if the money does not come through, you will have a serious problem. Overdrafts cause expensive fines and intentional overdrafts are <u>illegal!</u>

Include any loan repayments that you have as expenses and strive to pay those off as soon as feasible. You will want to pay off the highest interest loans and credit card debts as quickly as you can. Remember that check-cashing services (where they charge you money just to give you your own money sooner) are not good investments!!!

Coupons are good investments! Watch the papers for sales and coupons. The savings can add up quickly, if you stick to the products that you <u>normally</u> do buy. Loyalty cards that offer discounts at grocery stores are also free and can help keep costs down. Some of them trigger coupons based on what you frequently buy.

Credit cards that have no yearly fee and that offer a percent of your spending back to you ('cash back') can be good investments. Remember to treat the card balance as due in full each month so that you do not pay interest and finance charges. Research which cards offer incentives that fit with your lifestyle. A card that offers free airline miles, for instance, does not help if you never fly!

You may receive offers in the mail for new credit cards with surprisingly high credit limits. It may be tempting to just say 'yes' but remember that the more credit you have available, the higher the risk of becoming overextended. If you use that credit to live beyond your ability to repay the money, you end up paying enormous interest and finance charges. Try not to have more than a couple of different credit cards so that you will not be tempted to overextend your capability to pay. If you have ten, for instance, consider paying them off one by one and close all but a few. Less bills to pay!

One extremely important question for any budget is: Do I have the money for this? Ask yourself this *before* you buy it! If the answer is 'no' – then wait until you can afford it. It is as simple (and as complex) as that. Don't spend money that you don't have. <u>Really</u> wishing we could get our government to understand this concept! Teach your children how to manage money as they grow. This will be a valuable lesson to keep them financially stable from the outset.

Pay yourself first (whenever possible). This means to set aside some money for savings. This money is for unexpected expenses and for your future needs. The younger you are when you start saving money, the quicker it will add up. Even if it is just $25.00 per month, get used to doing this as soon as you can. Compounding interest adds up quickly in your favor. You can learn more about compounding interest online or talk to a bank.

Check out employer-matched savings programs. If your employer will match an amount set aside for savings, this can be greatly in your favor. Many employers have programs, possibly called deferred compensation, 401K or Individual Retirement Accounts (IRA). Employee benefits can tell you what, if anything, is available from your company. If your employer does not have this, you can still set up long-term savings on your own. Check into local bank programs.

It is important to set up savings at a young age. Social Security alone is not likely to provide a comfortable retirement. Each individual should have a Social Security account in their own name. You will each need to work a sufficient number of quarters to earn a Social Security retirement benefit. Be sure to monitor your progress with

Social Security to see that their information is complete and know how many quarters you have secured. They do occasionally have incomplete information and they will only go back a certain time period to correct it, so stay up to date. If you already have enough quarters, fine, but if you are going to be too short to obtain benefits, you probably want to consider working more hours before you retire (even part-time) not only for the additional income, but to build up the required number of quarters to be eligible for Social Security benefits when the time comes.

As your work life progresses, be checking into what retirement benefits you may be eligible for in addition to Social Security. There may be organizations such as Veteran's Benefits that you will be eligible to apply for and you may need to know in advance what the requirements are so that you can meet those requirements and not lose out on benefits because you needed to apply by a certain date, for instance.

Know where your money is going when you decide to contribute to a charity. Often a new world disaster brings out new scam artists to 'collect' for relief funds (that only relieve you of your money and none of it gets to the disaster victims). Do some research on the charity to see what percent of the donations go towards administration and what percent goes directly towards aid. Check what type of aid they actually provide. You may want to contribute through a church that you are familiar with, rather than an unknown charity.

5. CREDIT RATING

Establishing a good credit rating is important in maintaining good financial health. A poor credit rating will affect your ability to obtain a home loan, car loan or other types of credit. Landlords, employers, and insurance companies are also some of the people who consider your credit score when doing business with you.

There are three basic credit rating bureaus -Equifax, Experian and TransUnion. They track your credit status and report your ratings. They do occasionally have some wrong information, so if you obtain a report that has unfavorable incorrect information, there is a process for you to correct that information. You will need to contact the bureau.

Your credit rating will go up and down depending on many different things, one of which is late payments. Your credit rating suffers when you have late payments on your record from any source (car payment, house payment, credit card payment, etc.). Avoid late payments to keep from paying extra late fees as well as to keep your credit rating healthy.

How much credit and debt you have currently will also affect your credit score. If you have a large amount of debt compared to your income, that will lower your credit score (a higher credit score is better than a lower score). If you have a great deal of credit available to you, even if it isn't being used at the moment, that will also lower your score.

If you are just starting out on your own and need to establish a good credit rating, you will need to show that you can make payments on a balance (on time and consistently) and eventually pay the balance in full. It helps to start with a small credit card purchase and pay it off in full within a period of several months. Paying credit cards in full each month will be the goal after you have first established your ability to make monthly payments in a consistent timely manner.

You can check your present credit score through one of the three bureaus mentioned above. Each one allows one free credit report per year. You can stagger the three bureaus to obtain reports throughout the year (in four-month intervals for example) without paying for a report. You should see your credit score improve as you establish good financial habits.

When obtaining a free report, beware that you are not actually signing up for a paid service. Some online advertisements seem to be free but are actually obligating you to pay for something else, or to sign up to pay for subsequent reports – watch out for these.

Some credit cards will give you your credit score (without the detailed report) for no extra charge. Check with the credit card company, or their online site.

6. SOME "DOS AND DON'TS"

As you gain experience in managing your money, you will be able to add to this list on your own. For now, here are a few things to consider:

-Do know where your money is going and plan ahead for predictable increased needs down the line. For instance, if you know a certain expense increases every year, plan ahead to be able to cover that expense.

-Do establish a savings account. Don't spend all of your money just because you have it.

-Do check around for the best quality and prices. Don't overspend on items you can obtain elsewhere more reasonably (check discount stores over higher prices retail stores). Don't buy on impulse without checking prices.

-Do choose more affordable options wherever possible; do your research. Don't be unrealistic about what you 'need'.

-Do use coupons wherever possible. But, don't buy something you don't need just because there is a coupon!

-Do check out free entertainment (parks, libraries, walks, museums, family time at home). Don't pay for activities that you can find elsewhere for free (such as recreation centers, community activities, any free school activities).

-Do plan and 'work' your budget (and make adjustments as needed). Don't buy things you can't afford. Impulse control can save money! Take your time and think rationally about what you are purchasing.

-Do make food at home as often as you can. Soup, stew, casserole or salad at home are less expensive than eating out. Don't eat out if you can't afford it! Hold it down to a minimum and include the expense in your budget if you do eat out regularly.

-Do buy 'within your means'. Don't buy an expensive car if you can't afford it yet. More affordable cars take you the same places that a luxury car does.

-Do plan for upgrades in the future but buy what you can afford now. Be realistic about your budget. If you are just buying your first home, you don't necessarily need top-of-the-line. The more affordable homes are called 'starter homes' for a reason. Start modestly and upgrade as you are able. Consider the size that you need and location of the home realistically. School districts may be more important than size if you have school age children.

-Do take care of your possessions. Do maintenance on your cars routinely, don't wait for a problem to occur. Oil changes, brake checkups and tire rotations are cheaper than buying a new car or new tires.

-Do shop phone services: look for inexpensive plans and don't get locked into long expensive contracts. Pay-as-you-go plans can save a great deal of money if you are realistic about what you need – research the plans based on your specific needs.

-Do be careful about where you obtain tax services if you do not do your own tax forms. There are many different services available at a wide range of prices. You do want a reputable place (street vendors not recommended!) so, do some research before deciding. Also, don't wait until April 14th to fill out your forms. If you have to pay, you need some time to plan for the expense. If you are getting a refund, you want it as soon as possible.

If money is running tight in any given month, watch a movie at home on TV for free instead of going out to the movies. Cook a special dinner at home instead of going to a restaurant. Be up front about it with your family, they can help, and they need to learn about managing money too. You will be doing them a favor by teaching them to handle money from an early age.

Whether you are a one or two paycheck family, both spouses need to sit down together to plan the budget and each week to pay the bills. That way one person is not left with all the headache and all the responsibility. Have discussions together about budget issues. Whatever members your household consists of, all who are of an age to understand should be involved at some level. That way everyone is on the same page about spending, saving, and managing money.

A word about job interviews. Do put your best foot forward in an interview. Try to maintain a positive, helpful attitude and leave out any comments about how 'bad' your previous boss may have been. The new manager probably does not know you and will think that you are either a complainer or a problem employee yourself. While you do want to be yourself and be truthful, there is no reason to put forth a negative vibe. If you can't say anything good, don't say anything! Certainly do not lie, but you do not need to malign your current or former workplaces, either. Discretion is appreciated on both ends. 'Closer to home', 'better chance for advancement', 'this company has such a good reputation', or many other positive comments work better for a reason you are leaving your current employer, than 'I hate my job'!

If you are just starting out and looking for your first job, be aware that building a resume of work experience is important. You may not land your dream job at the very first try but be prepared to put in some time gaining experience. Any job that you have can provide some important experience in learning to be a part of the work force and dealing with bosses, managers and coworkers. Plus, it is usually easier to get a new job while you have a present job. Building up a work history helps you show a new employer that you are 'employable'. Of course, this does not mean job-hopping every two weeks – that does not look great on a resume!

Job satisfaction comes from within yourself, first. If you put forth your best effort and deal with others in a responsible way, you will know when you are doing a good job and that is a reward in itself. Getting a good review from your boss will be the icing on the cake.

7. SUMMARY

Don't become discouraged. As you pay attention to where your money is going, you will be more and more adept at making your money work for you.

Money worries are the worst. Plan ahead and avoid the stress that worrying about money can create. Being financially responsible contributes to good mental health. Even if you do not have much money, you can enjoy life much easier if you control your spending and stay out of debt.

It important to enjoy the 'here and now', too. You do want to allow yourself and your family to be happy. Just realize that money itself does not equal happiness. Many things that bring happiness are free. Life is a journey to be enjoyed daily, not just a destination to be reached someday.

ABOUT THE AUTHORS

Dennis Keegan is a retired Real Estate Broker and Gwen Keegan is a retired Registered Nurse. Together they have enjoyed owning and managing several small businesses in the past. They live in El Dorado Hills, California and enjoy family, friends, writing and traveling.

Made in the USA
Middletown, DE
04 September 2019